Pearl A. Taylor

The TRUTH About SANTA

A Warm and Honest Story Based on Saint Nicholas' Life

A long time ago,
there was a boy named Nicholas
who lived in a small town called Petra.
He was an ordinary boy,
but he had a heart as big as the sky.
He was kind, generous,
and always made people smile.

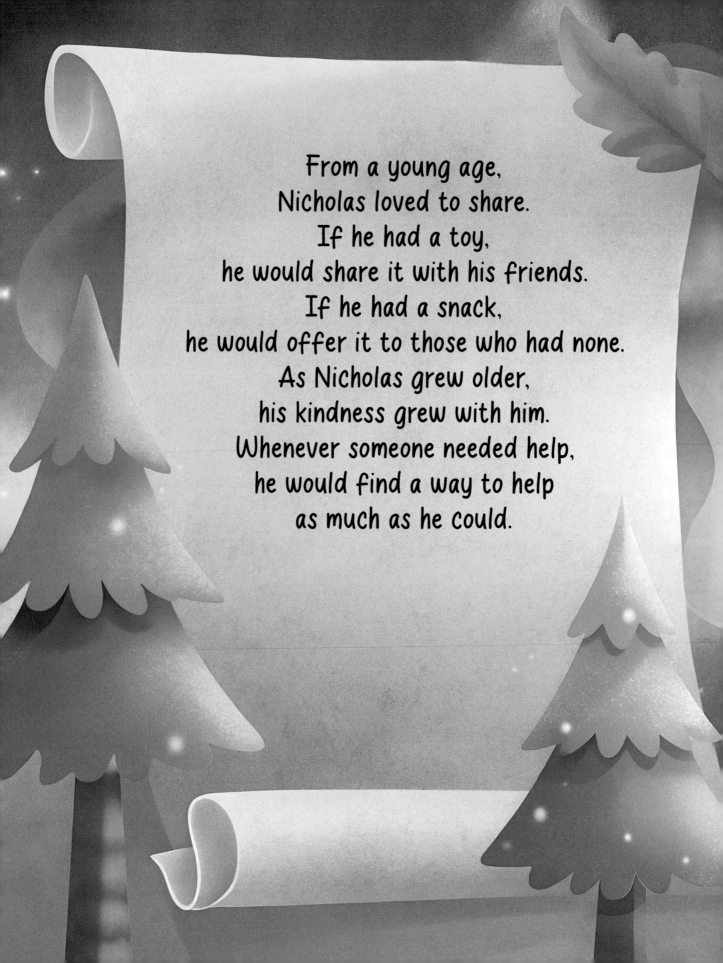

From a young age,
Nicholas loved to share.
If he had a toy,
he would share it with his friends.
If he had a snack,
he would offer it to those who had none.
As Nicholas grew older,
his kindness grew with him.
Whenever someone needed help,
he would find a way to help
as much as he could.

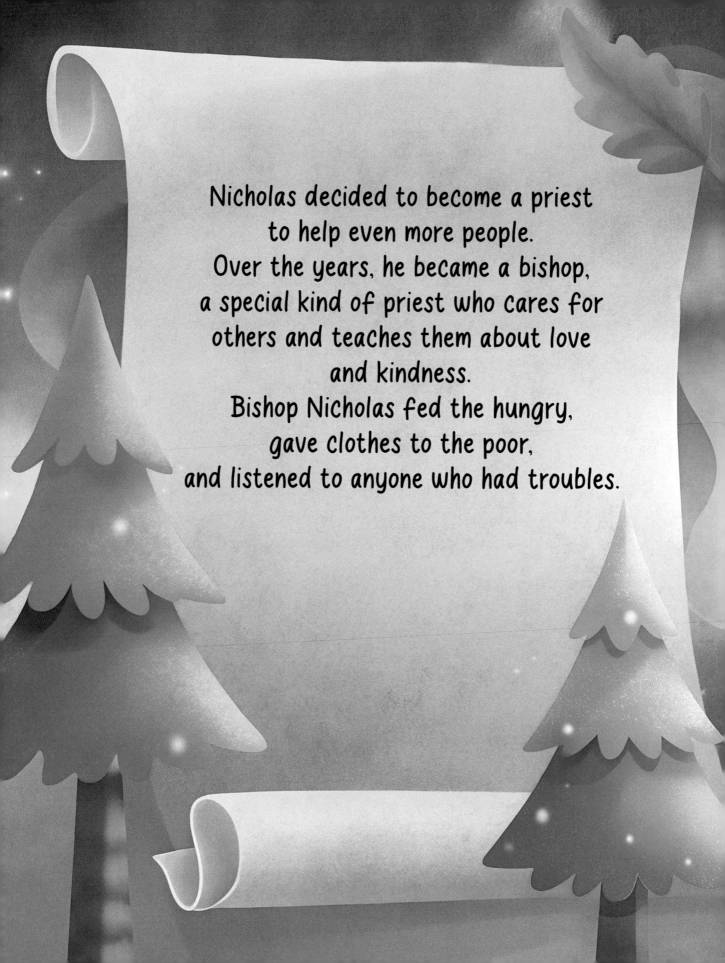

Nicholas decided to become a priest
to help even more people.
Over the years, he became a bishop,
a special kind of priest who cares for
others and teaches them about love
and kindness.
Bishop Nicholas fed the hungry,
gave clothes to the poor,
and listened to anyone who had troubles.

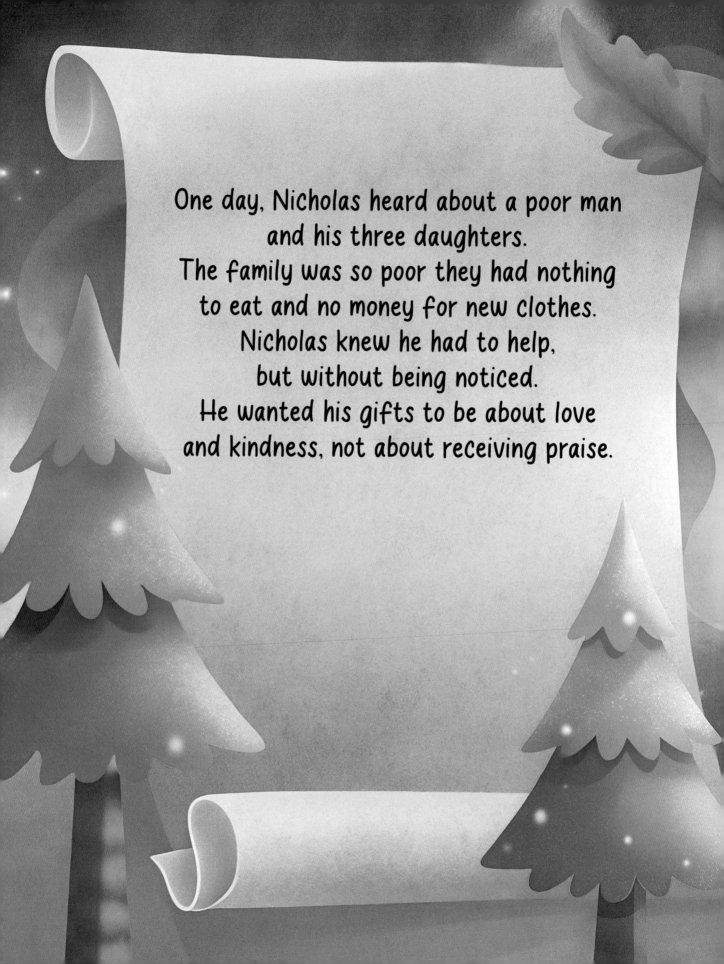

One day, Nicholas heard about a poor man
and his three daughters.
The family was so poor they had nothing
to eat and no money for new clothes.
Nicholas knew he had to help,
but without being noticed.
He wanted his gifts to be about love
and kindness, not about receiving praise.

That night, Nicholas filled
a small bag with gold coins.
He snuck over to the poor man's house
and tossed the bag down the chimney.
The coins fell into the stockings and shoes
that were drying by the fireplace.
That's how the tradition of Christmas
stockings and putting out shoes
to be filled with gifts began!

People began telling stories about the kind bishop who gave secret gifts and helped others. They called him Saint Nicholas because of his good deeds. When Nicholas passed away, people wanted to remember him, so they began to celebrate his life every year on December 6.

Over time, the stories
of Saint Nicholas spread even further
all around the world.
People in different countries started to
tell their own stories about him,
and Saint Nicholas became known as
Santa Claus.
His story evolved into magical tales,
creating the new tradition.

Santa Claus became a jolly figure
who gave gifts to children.
Tales were told about Santa
living at the North Pole
and making toys with elves
and delivering them to children
around the world.

On Christmas Eve, people said Santa
would fly in a sleigh pulled by reindeer,
bringing gifts to all the children
who had been good that year.
On Christmas morning,
children would wake up to find
presents left under the Christmas tree
by Santa Claus.

People all over the world began dressing up as Santa Claus, wearing the familiar red suit and white beard to bring joy to children during Christmas. These Santas are carrying on Saint Nicholas' spirit.
The real story of Saint Nicholas teaches us that the true magic of Christmas is kindness and generosity.

Santa Claus is a fun
and magical tradition that helps
keep the spirit of Saint Nicholas alive,
showing us that anyone,
regardless of age or background,
can spread goodness.
Even the smallest act of kindness
can make a big difference.

You don't need a red suit or a sleigh with reindeer to be like Santa. Here are some simple ways you can be like Saint Nicholas:

Be a Good Friend: When your friends are sad, be there for them. And when they're happy, celebrate with them! Being a good friend is one of the best ways to be kind.

Give to Those in Need: Gather old clothes, toys, or books you no longer use and donate them to a charity or someone in need. Every little bit helps and can bring a smile to someone's face.

Help at Home: Help your parents with chores or help your siblings when they need it. Helping out at home can show kindness, too!

Share Your Toys: You can share your toys with friends, neighbors, or children who might not have as many.

Spread Cheer: A simple "thank you" or a kind note can brighten someone's day.

Remember, the true spirit of Christmas
isn't about the gifts we receive,
but the love and kindness we share.
When you give a gift,
think about the happiness it will bring
to the person receiving it.
When you help someone, think about
how much it will mean to them.
Acts of kindness, no matter how small,
make the world a better place.

Imagine how wonderful the world
would be if everyone followed
the example of Saint Nicholas every day.
So, this Christmas and every day after,
remember that you can spread joy,
kindness, and love, making the world
a happier place for everyone.
The magic of Christmas is in the smiles,
the laughter, and the warmth
we share with each other.

And this is the true story
of Santa Claus.

Merry Christmas,
and remember to always be kind!

THE END

Thank you for picking up and reading my book!

If you enjoyed this book, I'd be incredibly grateful
if you could take a moment to leave an honest review.
Your feedback means the world to me,
and it helps me continue to create even better stories
for my readers.

Pearl A. Taylor

Scan here to leave a review:

Made in United States
Orlando, FL
16 November 2024

53952001R00022